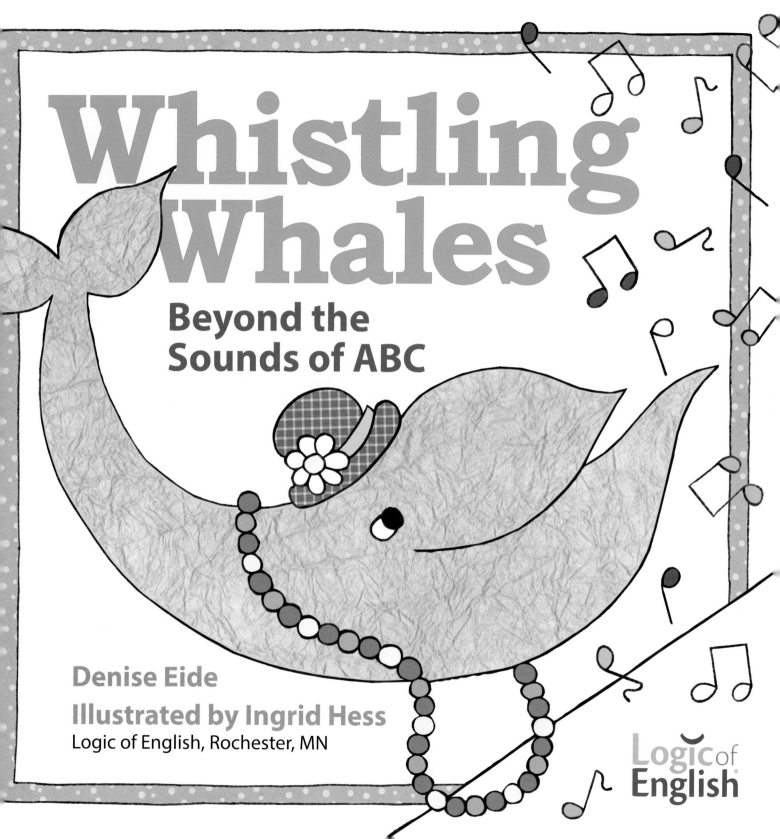

Whistling Whales

Beyond the Sounds of ABC

Denise Eide
Illustrated by Ingrid Hess
Logic of English, Rochester, MN

Logic of
English

Logic of English
4871 19th Street NW, Suite 110
Rochester, MN 55901

First Edition

Printed in the United States of America

ISBN 978-1-942154-13-6

10 9 8 7 6 5 4 3

www.LogicOfEnglish.com

Tips for Enjoying *Whistling Whales*

Help children develop an awareness that letters represent sounds.

- A phonogram is a picture of a sound. All words in English are written with a combination of phonograms. There are 74 basic phonograms.

- Point to the phonogram as you say the sound(s). Emphasize the sounds, not the letter names.

- This book introduces 21 multi-letter phonograms. These phonograms are taught in the Logic of English® curriculum *Foundations Level B*.

Sound Tips

- Many phonograms in English make additional sounds that are not commonly taught.

th	/th-TH/	think	this		
ch	/ch-k-sh/	chimp	school	charades	
ow	/ow-ō/	cow	glow		
ou	/ow-ō-ö-ŭ-ü/	pout	poultry	tour	country	should
ough	/ŏ-ō-ö-ow-ŭf-ŏf/	brought	dough	through	drought	enough	trough
ea	/ē-ĕ-ā/	tea	breakfast	bear

To hear the sounds: **www.LogicofEnglish.com/resources/phonogram-list**

Encourage your child's awareness of sounds!

4
+7
=
||

9
-4
5

th

/th-TH/

Think about this!

GO
SHARKS!

SHARKS
ROCK!

sh

/sh/

Sheepi**sh sh**arks wa**sh**ing **sh**ips.

ck

/k/

A lu**ck**y du**ck** drives a tru**ck**.

igh

/ī/

Kn**igh**ts f**igh**t with br**igh**t l**igh**ts.

1 2 3 4 5 6 7

ch

/ch-k-sh/

Chimps at s**ch**ool
play **ch**arades.

ee

/ē/

Beep! Beep!
Sheep in the street.

er

/er/

Fiddlers and farmers
fill the chopper.

wh

/wh/

Whistling **wh**ales **wh**irl and twirl.

oy

/oi/

Boys depl**oy** trucks with j**oy**.

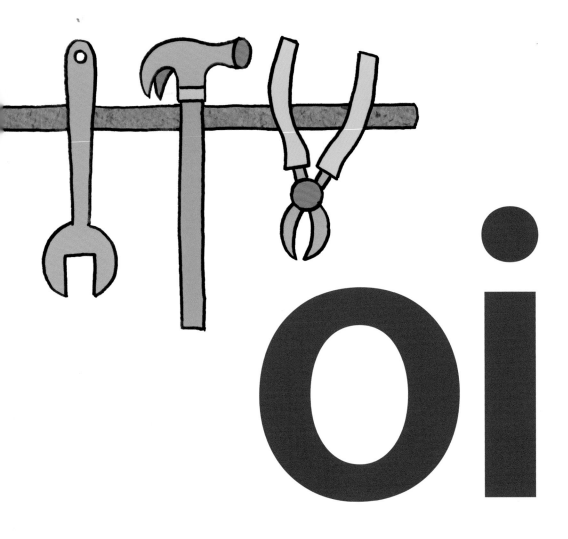

oi

/oi/

Oil those j**oi**nts! Av**oi**d the n**oi**se!

ay

/ā/

Get away!
The archway sways.

ai

/ā/

All hail! Snail mail!

ng

/ng/

Di**ng**! Do**ng**! Ba**ng** the go**ng**!

ar

/ar/

Sta**rt** the **car**! The p**ar**ty's **far**!

/or/

Storks escort her
through the storm.

tch

/ch/

Wa**tch** and ske**tch** the hopsco**tch** ma**tch**.

ow

/ow-ō/

Cows that row. Gowns that glow.

ou

/ow-ō-ö-ŭ-ü/

Po**u**ting **p**o**u**ltry sh**ou**ld **t**o**u**r the **c**o**u**ntry.

ough

/ŏ-ō-ö-ow-ŭf-ŏf/

She brought dough through the drought
and had enough in her trough.

ea

/ē-ĕ-ā/

Tea for br**ea**kfast with a b**ea**r.

oa

/ō/

The g**oa**t in the b**oa**t
just ate my c**oa**t!

Other Products by Logic of English

- **Doodling Dragons: An ABC Book of Sounds**

- **Knitting Knights: Beyond the Sounds of ABC**

- **Uncovering the Logic of English: A Common-Sense Approach to Reading, Spelling, and Literacy**

- **Logic of English Foundations Curriculum**
  A Reading, Spelling and Writing Program for Ages 4-7
  Levels A, B, C, and D

- **Foundations Readers**
  Levels B, C, and D

- **Logic of English Essentials Curriculum**
  Multi-Level Reading, Spelling, Grammar & Vocabulary

- **The Essentials Reader**

- **Phonogram and Spelling Game Book**

- **Phonogram Game Cards**

- **Phonogram Game Tiles**

- **Phonogram Flash Cards**

- **Spelling Rule Flash Cards**

- **Rhythm of Handwriting Series**

www.LogicOfEnglish.com